Siberian
Survivor

PIONEER EDITION

By Rene Ebersole

CONTENTS

By Rene Ebersole

Siberian Survivor

This is a Siberian tiger. It is a comeback cat. Studies show more are living in the wild.

Howard Quigley has been hunted. He's been hunted by a jaguar. He has been chased by a black bear. Yet he was most scared when he met Olga. She is a Siberian tiger.

Purr-fect Meeting

Olga saw him. She roared. What would she do? Quigley did not know. Would she run away? Or would she attack?

Quigley is a **biologist**. That's a scientist who studies animals. He stayed calm. Slowly he aimed his gun at the tiger. He shot a dart at the cat.

Bulls-eye! The dart hit Olga. She stumbled. She fell down. She was asleep.

Cat Paws. *Tigers have five toes on their front feet. They have four toes on their back feet.* INSET: *Biologists study a tiger in the wild.*

Cat Tracks

Quigley went to work. The cat slept. He took blood samples. He checked Olga's heartbeat. He measured her body.

Quigley also put a **radio collar** on her neck. The collar sends out beeps. The beeps tell when Olga is sleeping. Or when she is hunting. Collars show people what the tiger does.

Saving Siberians

Quigley needs to learn all he can about Olga. Why? He wants to keep tigers from dying out forever.

Three kinds of tigers have died out. Only five kinds of tigers are left. That includes Siberian tigers.

Dangers in the Wild

Siberian tigers once lived from Russia to South Korea. By 1900, fewer than 50 tigers were left! People had killed most of them.

People still hunt tigers today. Why? Some kill tigers to make medicines. They think tiger parts heal people. Others hunt tigers for money. They are called **poachers**. They hunt illegally.

They can get about $15,000 for one dead tiger in Asia. That's more money than most Asian families make in several years.

Open Wide. *A tiger sticks out its tongue. It gather scents this way. It tastes its tongue. This tells a tiger the direction a scent came from. This is called flehmening.*

4

High Climber. *Siberian tigers can climb trees. Just like a house cat!*

Losing Forests

Poaching is bad. But tigers face other dangers. They are losing their forest **habitat**, or home.

The largest forest on the planet is in Russia. A third of all trees in the world grow there. Siberian tigers live there, too. So do the animals they hunt. Today, people are cutting down many of the trees. This destroys the tigers' habitat.

Living Together

Quigley thinks people and tigers can live together. Some trees can be cut down. Others can be left standing. This would let people and tigers use the same forests.

Protecting tiger habitat could even help people make money. People could visit the forests to see tigers. This would create jobs. So people wouldn't need to poach.

Tiger Facts

- 🐾 Tigers live in the wild only in Asia.

- 🐾 Female tigers usually give birth to two or three cubs at a time.

- 🐾 A newborn cub weighs between 2 and 3 pounds.

- 🐾 An adult male tiger weighs up to 550 pounds.

- 🐾 Tigers and other big cats can roar. But they cannot purr.

- 🐾 Tigers are one of the few cats that like to swim in water.

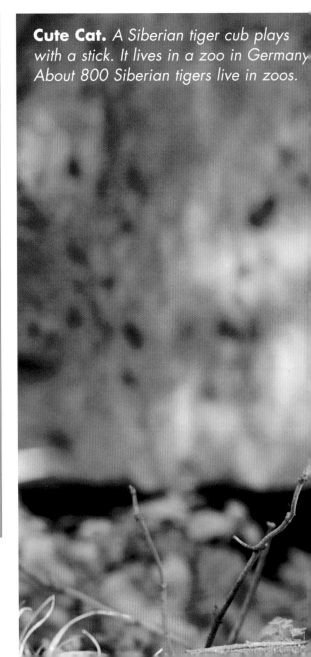

Cute Cat. A Siberian tiger cub plays with a stick. It lives in a zoo in Germany. About 800 Siberian tigers live in zoos.

Tiger Triumph?

Some tigers are still hunted. Their habitat is still getting smaller. But there is hope. The number of Siberian tigers is on the rise. Nearly 400 may now live in the wild.

That may not sound like a lot. Yet it is a start. There are more tigers alive today than there were 100 years ago. Tigers may survive in the wild after all.

Wordwise

biologist: scientist who studies life
habitat: place where plants and animals live
poacher: illegal hunter
radio collar: machine used to track animals

Tiger Types

Five species, or kinds, of tigers are still alive today. They all look similar. However, their stripes form different patterns. The species are also different sizes.

Bengal

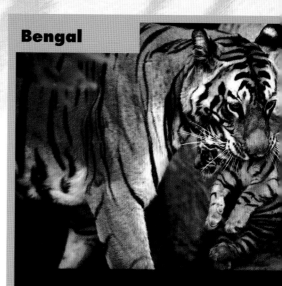

Size Male Bengal tigers are about 9 feet long. They weigh almost 500 pounds.

Diet Bengal tigers eat mainly wild cattle and deer.

Population Scientists think 3,000 to 5,000 Bengal tigers live in the wild.

It is a fact! Some Bengal tigers are white with black stripes. White tigers are very rare. None have been seen in the wild since the 1950s!

Siberian

Size Siberian tigers are the world's biggest cats. Males can be more than 10 feet long. They weigh more than 600 pounds.

Diet Siberian tigers eat mostly elk and wild boar.

Population Scientists think that there are fewer than 400 Siberian tigers left in the wild.

It is a fact! Siberian tigers have thick coats. Their fur is the thickest of any tiger. Winters get very cold where they live. Their thick fur keeps them warm.

dochinese

Size Male Indochinese tigers can be about 9 feet long. They weigh up to 400 pounds.

Diet They eat wild pigs. They eat wild cattle. They eat deer.

Population Scientists think that fewer than 2,000 Indochinese tigers are left in the world.

It is a fact! Some stripes on these tigers are spots. This is one way they look different from other tigers.

Sumatran

Size Sumatran tigers are the smallest tigers. The males are about 8 feet long. They weigh less than 300 pounds.

Diet Sumatran tigers eat wild pigs and deer.

Population Scientists think that only about 400 Sumatran tigers live in the wild.

It is a fact! Sumatran tigers are found only on the island of Sumatra. Most of these tigers live in national parks.

outh China

Size Male South China tigers are about 8 feet long. They weigh about 330 pounds.

Diet Very little is known about what these tigers eat in the wild. That is because so few have been seen.

Population No one has seen a wild South China tiger in 20 years.

It is a fact! The South China tiger is the rarest tiger. Fewer than 60 South China tigers are known to be alive in zoos.

EUROPE

URAL MOUNTAINS

Ob River

Irtysh River

Yenisey River

Lena River

Amur River

Lake Baikal

Aral Sea

ASIA

TIAN SHAN

GOBI

Yellow River

HIMALAYA

Indus River

Brahmaputra

Yangtze River

Ganges River

Mekong River

Bay of Bengal

South China Sea

Sumatra

Borneo

INDIAN OCEAN

Map Key

Mountain		Grassland	
Desert		Wetland	
Coniferous forest		Tundra	
Deciduous forest		Volcano	
Rain forest		Tiger ranges	

T•Land of the Tiger

In the wild, tigers live only in Asia. They are found in many kinds of habitats. They live in swamps. They live in marshes. They live in steamy rain forests. They live in cold spruce forests. All they need is shade, water, food, and space. They need lots of space. Tigers need land for hunting. They eat antelope. They eat deer. They eat wild pigs. And they eat other large animals. They can eat 50 pounds of meal in a night.

VOLODYMYR BURDIAK/SHUTTERSTOCK.COM

	Tiger	Number in the wild	Characteristics
🐾	Bengal	3,159–4,715	Some Bengal tigers are white.
🐾	Indochinese	1,227–1,785	These are smaller and darker than Bengals.
🐾	Siberian	about 400	Siberian tigers are the largest cats in the world.
🐾	South China	fewer than 60	This tiger has short, widely spaced stripes.
🐾	Sumatran	about 400	The darkest tiger has closely spaced stripes.

ATIONAL GEOGRAPHIC MAPS

Tigers

It is time to track down what you learned about tigers.

1 How do radio collars help biologists study tigers?

2 Why do people hunt tigers?

3 Describe a tiger's habitat.

4 How do the five kinds of tigers alive today compare?

5 Are wild tigers surviving better today than in the past? Explain.